# The *Intentional Life* Journal

D1521003

By Destini Edmond

_This Journal Belongs to:_

_____

# Dedication

This journal is dedicated to all of the women that have shown up for every one else time and time again but are ready to show up for themselves now.

It's your turn.

I am
intentional.

date: ___/___/___

Sleep Tracker: _____ hours

S M T W T F S

Mood Tracker: ☺ 😐 🙁 😣

Today's Affirmation:

What am I looking forward to?

_____

_____

My top 3 to-dos:                    Done

1. _____  ☐

2. _____  ☐

3. _____  ☐

What will it take to get these done?

_____

_____

I am grateful for:

_____

_____

date: __/__/__

Rate my day: ☆ ☆ ☆ ☆ ☆

S M T W T F S

My favorite part of the day was...

_____

One thing I would change is...

_____

I am going to refill my cup by...

_____

_____

What I'll do tonight to prepare for tomorrow...

_____

_____

Tomorrow's morning routine will look like:

In bed by:_____    Alarm set for:_____

date: ___/___/___

Sleep Tracker: _____ hours

S M T W T F S

Mood Tracker: ☺ 😐 ☹ 😠

Today's Affirmation:

What am I looking forward to?

My top 3 to-dos:                                          Done

1. _____ ☐

2. _____ ☐

3. _____ ☐

What will it take to get these done?

I am grateful for:

date: __/__/__

Rate my day: ☆ ☆ ☆ ☆ ☆

S M T W T F S

My favorite part of the day was...

_____

One thing I would change is...

_____

I am going to refill my cup by...

_____

_____

What I'll do tonight to prepare for tomorrow...

_____

_____

Tomorrow's morning routine will look like:

In bed by:_____     Alarm set for: _____

date: ___/___/___

Sleep Tracker: _____ hours

S  M  T  W  T  F  S

Mood Tracker: ☺ 😐 ☹ 😣

### Today's Affirmation:

What am I looking forward to?

_____

_____

My top 3 to-dos:                                    Done

1. _____  ☐

2. _____  ☐

3. _____  ☐

What will it take to get these done?

_____

_____

I am grateful for:

_____

_____

☾

date: ___/___/___

Rate my day: ☆ ☆ ☆ ☆ ☆

S M T W T F S

My favorite part of the day was...

_____

One thing I would change is...

_____

I am going to refill my cup by...

_____

_____

What I'll do tonight to prepare for tomorrow...

_____

_____

Tomorrow's morning routine will look like:

In bed by:_____    Alarm set for: _____

date: __/__/__

Sleep Tracker: _____ hours

S M T W T F S

Mood Tracker: ☺ 😐 🙁 😖

Today's Affirmation:

What am I looking forward to?

My top 3 to-dos:                                    Done

1.                                                          ☐

2.                                                          ☐

3.                                                          ☐

What will it take to get these done?

I am grateful for:

date: ___/___/___

Rate my day: ☆ ☆ ☆ ☆ ☆

S M T W T F S

My favorite part of the day was...

_____

One thing I would change is...

_____

I am going to refill my cup by...

_____

_____

What I'll do tonight to prepare for tomorrow...

_____

_____

Tomorrow's morning routine will look like:

In bed by:_____    Alarm set for: _____

date: ___/___/___

Sleep Tracker: _____ hours

S M T W T F S

Mood Tracker: ☺ 😐 ☹ 😠

## Today's Affirmation:

What am I looking forward to?

_____

_____

My top 3 to-dos:                                    Done

1. _____  ☐

2. _____  ☐

3. _____  ☐

What will it take to get these done?

_____

_____

I am grateful for:

_____

_____

☾

Rate my day: ☆ ☆ ☆ ☆ ☆          S M T W T F S

My favorite part of the day was...

_____

One thing I would change is...

_____

I am going to refill my cup by...

_____

_____

What I'll do tonight to prepare for tomorrow...

_____

_____

Tomorrow's morning routine will look like:

In bed by:_____     Alarm set for: _____

date: ___/___/___

Sleep Tracker: _____ hours

S M T W T F S

Mood Tracker: ☺ 😐 ☹ 😣

Today's Affirmation:

What am I looking forward to?

_____

_____

My top 3 to-dos:                                    Done

1. _____  ☐

2. _____  ☐

3. _____  ☐

What will it take to get these done?

_____

_____

I am grateful for:

_____

_____

date: ___/___/___

Rate my day: ☆ ☆ ☆ ☆ ☆

S M T W T F S

My favorite part of the day was...

_____

One thing I would change is...

_____

I am going to refill my cup by...

_____

_____

What I'll do tonight to prepare for tomorrow...

_____

_____

Tomorrow's morning routine will look like:

In bed by:_____ Alarm set for: _____

date: __/__/__

Sleep Tracker: _____ hours

S  M  T  W  T  F  S

Mood Tracker: ☺ 😐 ☹ 😠

Today's Affirmation:

What am I looking forward to?

_____

_____

My top 3 to-dos:                                    Done

1. _____  ☐

2. _____  ☐

3. _____  ☐

What will it take to get these done?

_____

_____

I am grateful for:

_____

_____

Rate my day: ☆ ☆ ☆ ☆ ☆

My favorite part of the day was...

_____

One thing I would change is...

_____

I am going to refill my cup by...

_____

_____

What I'll do tonight to prepare for tomorrow...

_____

_____

Tomorrow's morning routine will look like:

In bed by:____    Alarm set for: ____

# Weekly Recap

date: ___/___/___

I feel...

Healthy   Accomplished   Spiritual   Creative   Satisfied

What did I do that helped me make the best use of my time?

_____

_____

How could I have maximized my time more?

_____

_____

What did I learn?

_____

_____

How will I improve next week?

_____

_____

Reflections:

_____

_____

I am
focused.

date: __/__/__

Sleep Tracker: _____ hours

S  M  T  W  T  F  S

Mood Tracker:  ☺  😐  🙁  😫

Today's Affirmation:

What am I looking forward to?

_____

_____

My top 3 to-dos:                                    Done

   1. _____  ☐

   2. _____  ☐

   3. _____  ☐

What will it take to get these done?

_____

_____

I am grateful for:

_____

_____

Rate my day: ☆ ☆ ☆ ☆ ☆

date: __/__/__

S M T W T F S

My favorite part of the day was...

_____

One thing I would change is...

_____

I am going to refill my cup by...

_____

_____

What I'll do tonight to prepare for tomorrow...

_____

_____

Tomorrow's morning routine will look like:

In bed by:_____    Alarm set for:_____

date: __/__/__

Sleep Tracker: _____ hours

S  M  T  W  T  F  S

Mood Tracker:  ☺  😐  🙁  😠

## Today's Affirmation:

What am I looking forward to?

_____

_____

My top 3 to-dos:                    Done

1. _____  ☐

2. _____  ☐

3. _____  ☐

What will it take to get these done?

_____

_____

I am grateful for:

_____

_____

date: ___/___/___

Rate my day: ☆ ☆ ☆ ☆ ☆

S M T W T F S

My favorite part of the day was...

_____

One thing I would change is...

_____

I am going to refill my cup by...

_____

_____

What I'll do tonight to prepare for tomorrow...

_____

_____

Tomorrow's morning routine will look like:

In bed by:_____    Alarm set for:_____

date: __/__/__

Sleep Tracker: _____ hours

S M T W T F S

Mood Tracker: ☺ 😐 ☹ 😫

### Today's Affirmation:

What am I looking forward to?

_____

_____

My top 3 to-dos:                                    Done

1. _____  ☐

2. _____  ☐

3. _____  ☐

What will it take to get these done?

_____

_____

I am grateful for:

_____

_____

date: ___/___/___

Rate my day: ☆ ☆ ☆ ☆ ☆

S M T W T F S

My favorite part of the day was...

_____

One thing I would change is...

_____

I am going to refill my cup by...

_____

_____

What I'll do tonight to prepare for tomorrow...

_____

_____

Tomorrow's morning routine will look like:

In bed by:_____    Alarm set for: _____

date: __/__/__

Sleep Tracker: _____ hours

S M T W T F S

Mood Tracker: ☺ 😐 ☹ 😣

Today's Affirmation:

What am I looking forward to?

_____

_____

My top 3 to-dos:                                    Done

1. _____ ☐

2. _____ ☐

3. _____ ☐

What will it take to get these done?

_____

_____

I am grateful for:

_____

_____

date: ___/___/___

Rate my day: ☆ ☆ ☆ ☆ ☆

S M T W T F S

My favorite part of the day was...

_____

One thing I would change is...

_____

I am going to refill my cup by...

_____

_____

What I'll do tonight to prepare for tomorrow...

_____

_____

Tomorrow's morning routine will look like:

In bed by:_____    Alarm set for:_____

date: __/__/__

Sleep Tracker: _____ hours

S  M  T  W  T  F  S

Mood Tracker: ☺ 😐 ☹ 😠

Today's Affirmation:

What am I looking forward to?

_____

_____

My top 3 to-dos:                                    Done

1. _____  ☐

2. _____  ☐

3. _____  ☐

What will it take to get these done?

_____

_____

I am grateful for:

_____

_____

date: __/__/__

Rate my day: ☆ ☆ ☆ ☆ ☆

S M T W T F S

My favorite part of the day was...

_____

One thing I would change is...

_____

I am going to refill my cup by...

_____

_____

What I'll do tonight to prepare for tomorrow...

_____

_____

Tomorrow's morning routine will look like:

In bed by:_____    Alarm set for:_____

date: __/__/__

Sleep Tracker: _____ hours

Mood Tracker: 😊 😐 🙁 😠

S  M  T  W  T  F  S

Today's Affirmation:

What am I looking forward to?

_____

_____

My top 3 to-dos:                                    Done

1. _____  ☐

2. _____  ☐

3. _____  ☐

What will it take to get these done?

_____

_____

I am grateful for:

_____

_____

☾

date: ___/___/___

Rate my day: ☆ ☆ ☆ ☆ ☆

S M T W T F S

My favorite part of the day was...

_____

One thing I would change is...

_____

I am going to refill my cup by...

_____

_____

What I'll do tonight to prepare for tomorrow...

_____

_____

Tomorrow's morning routine will look like:

In bed by:____    Alarm set for: ____

date: ___/___/___

Sleep Tracker: _____ hours

S  M  T  W  T  F  S

Mood Tracker: ☺ 😐 🙁 😣

Today's Affirmation:

What am I looking forward to?

My top 3 to-dos:                                    Done

1. _____    ☐

2. _____    ☐

3. _____    ☐

What will it take to get these done?

I am grateful for:

date: __ / __ / __

Rate my day: ☆ ☆ ☆ ☆ ☆

S M T W T F S

My favorite part of the day was...

_____

One thing I would change is...

_____

I am going to refill my cup by...

_____

_____

What I'll do tonight to prepare for tomorrow...

_____

_____

Tomorrow's morning routine will look like:

In bed by:_____     Alarm set for:_____

# Weekly Recap

date: ___/___/___

I feel...

Healthy  Accomplished  Spiritual  Creative  Satisfied

What did I do that helped me make the best use of my time?

_____

_____

How could I have maximized my time more?

_____

_____

What did I learn?

_____

_____

How will I improve next week?

_____

_____

Reflections:

_____

_____

I am
balanced.

date: __/__/__

Sleep Tracker: _____ hours

S M T W T F S

Mood Tracker: ☺ ☺ ☹ ☹

Today's Affirmation:

What am I looking forward to?

_____

_____

My top 3 to-dos:                                 Done

1. _____  ☐

2. _____  ☐

3. _____  ☐

What will it take to get these done?

_____

_____

I am grateful for:

_____

_____

date: ___/___/___

Rate my day: ☆ ☆ ☆ ☆ ☆

S M T W T F S

My favorite part of the day was...

_____

One thing I would change is...

_____

I am going to refill my cup by...

_____

_____

What I'll do tonight to prepare for tomorrow...

_____

_____

Tomorrow's morning routine will look like:

In bed by:_____     Alarm set for: _____

date: __/__/__

Sleep Tracker: _____ hours

S M T W T F S

Mood Tracker: ☺ 😐 🙁 😠

Today's Affirmation:

What am I looking forward to?

_____

_____

My top 3 to-dos:                                    Done

1. _____  ☐

2. _____  ☐

3. _____  ☐

What will it take to get these done?

_____

_____

I am grateful for:

_____

_____

☾

Rate my day: ☆ ☆ ☆ ☆ ☆

S M T W T F S

My favorite part of the day was...

_____

One thing I would change is...

_____

I am going to refill my cup by...

_____

_____

What I'll do tonight to prepare for tomorrow...

_____

_____

Tomorrow's morning routine will look like:

In bed by:_____     Alarm set for: _____

date: ___/___/___

Sleep Tracker: _____ hours

S  M  T  W  T  F  S

Mood Tracker:  ☺  ☺  ☹  ☹

## Today's Affirmation:

What am I looking forward to?

_____

_____

My top 3 to-dos:                                    Done

1. _____  ☐

2. _____  ☐

3. _____  ☐

What will it take to get these done?

_____

_____

I am grateful for:

_____

_____

Rate my day: ☆ ☆ ☆ ☆ ☆

date: __/__/__

S M T W T F S

My favorite part of the day was...

_____

One thing I would change is...

_____

I am going to refill my cup by...

_____

_____

What I'll do tonight to prepare for tomorrow...

_____

_____

Tomorrow's morning routine will look like:

In bed by:____     Alarm set for: ____

date: __/__/__

Sleep Tracker: _____ hours

S M T W T F S

Mood Tracker: 😊 😐 🙁 😠

### Today's Affirmation:

What am I looking forward to?

_____

_____

My top 3 to-dos:                                    Done

1. _____   ☐

2. _____   ☐

3. _____   ☐

What will it take to get these done?

_____

_____

I am grateful for:

_____

_____

date: __/__/__

Rate my day: ☆ ☆ ☆ ☆ ☆

S M T W T F S

My favorite part of the day was...

_____

One thing I would change is...

_____

I am going to refill my cup by...

_____

_____

What I'll do tonight to prepare for tomorrow...

_____

_____

Tomorrow's morning routine will look like:

In bed by:_____    Alarm set for: _____

date: ___/___/___

Sleep Tracker: _____ hours

S M T W T F S

Mood Tracker: ☺ 😐 ☹ 😣

Today's Affirmation:

What am I looking forward to?

_____

_____

My top 3 to-dos:                                    Done

1. _____     ☐

2. _____     ☐

3. _____     ☐

What will it take to get these done?

_____

_____

I am grateful for:

_____

_____

date: ___/___/___

Rate my day: ☆ ☆ ☆ ☆ ☆

S M T W T F S

My favorite part of the day was...

_____

One thing I would change is...

_____

I am going to refill my cup by...

_____

_____

What I'll do tonight to prepare for tomorrow...

_____

_____

Tomorrow's morning routine will look like:

In bed by:_____    Alarm set for:_____

date: __ / __ / __

Sleep Tracker: _____ hours

S M T W T F S

Mood Tracker: ☺ 😐 ☹ 😠

Today's Affirmation:

What am I looking forward to?

_____

_____

My top 3 to-dos:                                    Done

1. _____ ☐

2. _____ ☐

3. _____ ☐

What will it take to get these done?

_____

_____

I am grateful for:

_____

_____

date: __/__/__

Rate my day: ☆ ☆ ☆ ☆ ☆

S M T W T F S

My favorite part of the day was...

_____

One thing I would change is...

_____

I am going to refill my cup by...

_____

_____

What I'll do tonight to prepare for tomorrow...

_____

_____

Tomorrow's morning routine will look like:

In bed by:_____    Alarm set for:_____

date: __/__/__

Sleep Tracker: _____ hours

S M T W T F S

Mood Tracker: ☺ 😐 ☹ 😣

Today's Affirmation:

What am I looking forward to?

_____

_____

My top 3 to-dos:                    Done

1. _____    ☐

2. _____    ☐

3. _____    ☐

What will it take to get these done?

_____

_____

I am grateful for:

_____

_____

date: ___/___/___

Rate my day: ☆ ☆ ☆ ☆ ☆

S M T W T F S

My favorite part of the day was...

_____

One thing I would change is...

_____

I am going to refill my cup by...

_____

_____

What I'll do tonight to prepare for tomorrow...

_____

_____

Tomorrow's morning routine will look like:

In bed by:_____     Alarm set for: _____

# Weekly Recap

date: ___/___/___

I feel...

Healthy   Accomplished   Spiritual   Creative   Satisfied

What did I do that helped me make the best use of my time?

_____

_____

How could I have maximized my time more?

_____

_____

What did I learn?

_____

_____

How will I improve next week?

_____

_____

Reflections:

_____

_____

I am
growing.

date: __/__/__

Sleep Tracker: _____ hours

S M T W T F S

Mood Tracker: 🙂 😐 🙁 😠

## Today's Affirmation:

## What am I looking forward to?

_____

_____

My top 3 to-dos:                                      Done

  1. _____ ☐

  2. _____ ☐

  3. _____ ☐

## What will it take to get these done?

_____

_____

## I am grateful for:

_____

_____

date: ___/___/___

Rate my day: ☆ ☆ ☆ ☆ ☆

S M T W T F S

My favorite part of the day was...

_____

One thing I would change is...

_____

I am going to refill my cup by...

_____

_____

What I'll do tonight to prepare for tomorrow...

_____

_____

Tomorrow's morning routine will look like:

In bed by:_____     Alarm set for: _____

date: __/__/__

Sleep Tracker: _____ hours

Mood Tracker: ☺ 😐 ☹ 😠

### Today's Affirmation:

What am I looking forward to?

_____

_____

My top 3 to-dos:                                    Done

1. _____  ☐

2. _____  ☐

3. _____  ☐

What will it take to get these done?

_____

_____

I am grateful for:

_____

_____

date: __/__/__

Rate my day: ☆ ☆ ☆ ☆ ☆          S M T W T F S

My favorite part of the day was...

_____

One thing I would change is...

_____

I am going to refill my cup by...

_____

_____

What I'll do tonight to prepare for tomorrow...

_____

_____

Tomorrow's morning routine will look like:

In bed by:_____    Alarm set for: _____

date: __/__/__

Sleep Tracker: _____ hours

S M T W T F S

Mood Tracker: ☺ 😐 ☹ 😖

## Today's Affirmation:

What am I looking forward to?

_____

_____

My top 3 to-dos:                                    Done

1. _____  ☐

2. _____  ☐

3. _____  ☐

What will it take to get these done?

_____

_____

I am grateful for:

_____

_____

☾

date: __/__/__

Rate my day: ☆ ☆ ☆ ☆ ☆

S M T W T F S

My favorite part of the day was...

_____

One thing I would change is...

_____

I am going to refill my cup by...

_____

_____

What I'll do tonight to prepare for tomorrow...

_____

_____

Tomorrow's morning routine will look like:

In bed by:_____    Alarm set for: _____

date: __/__/__

Sleep Tracker: _____ hours

S M T W T F S

Mood Tracker:  😊  😐  🙁  😣

## Today's Affirmation:

What am I looking forward to?

_____

_____

My top 3 to-dos:                          Done

1. _____  ☐

2. _____  ☐

3. _____  ☐

What will it take to get these done?

_____

_____

I am grateful for:

_____

_____

date: __/__/__

Rate my day: ☆ ☆ ☆ ☆ ☆          S M T W T F S

My favorite part of the day was...

_____

One thing I would change is...

_____

I am going to refill my cup by...

_____

_____

What I'll do tonight to prepare for tomorrow...

_____

_____

Tomorrow's morning routine will look like:

In bed by:_____     Alarm set for:_____

date: ___/___/___

Sleep Tracker: _____ hours

S  M  T  W  T  F  S

Mood Tracker: 😊 😐 🙁 😣

## Today's Affirmation:

What am I looking forward to?

_____

_____

My top 3 to-dos:                                    Done

1. _____  ☐

2. _____  ☐

3. _____  ☐

What will it take to get these done?

_____

_____

I am grateful for:

_____

_____

date: ___/___/___

Rate my day: ☆ ☆ ☆ ☆ ☆

S M T W T F S

My favorite part of the day was...

_____

One thing I would change is...

_____

I am going to refill my cup by...

_____

_____

What I'll do tonight to prepare for tomorrow...

_____

_____

Tomorrow's morning routine will look like:

In bed by:_____     Alarm set for: _____

date: __/__/__

Sleep Tracker: _____ hours

S  M  T  W  T  F  S

Mood Tracker: ☺ 😐 ☹ 😣

## Today's Affirmation:

What am I looking forward to?

_____

_____

My top 3 to-dos:                                        Done

1. _____  ☐

2. _____  ☐

3. _____  ☐

What will it take to get these done?

_____

_____

I am grateful for:

_____

_____

☾

date: ___/___/___

Rate my day: ☆ ☆ ☆ ☆ ☆

S M T W T F S

My favorite part of the day was...

_____

One thing I would change is...

_____

I am going to refill my cup by...

_____

_____

What I'll do tonight to prepare for tomorrow...

_____

_____

Tomorrow's morning routine will look like:

In bed by:_____    Alarm set for: _____

date: __/__/__

Sleep Tracker: _____ hours

S M T W T F S

Mood Tracker: ☺ ☺ ☹ ☹

Today's Affirmation:

What am I looking forward to?

_____

_____

My top 3 to-dos:                                        Done

1. _____ ☐

2. _____ ☐

3. _____ ☐

What will it take to get these done?

_____

_____

I am grateful for:

_____

_____

☾

date: ___/___/___

Rate my day: ☆ ☆ ☆ ☆ ☆

S M T W T F S

My favorite part of the day was...

_____

One thing I would change is...

_____

I am going to refill my cup by...

_____

_____

What I'll do tonight to prepare for tomorrow...

_____

_____

Tomorrow's morning routine will look like:

In bed by:_____    Alarm set for: _____

# Weekly Recap

date: ___/___/___

I feel...

Healthy   Accomplished   Spiritual   Creative   Satisfied

What did I do that helped me make the best use of my time?

_____

_____

How could I have maximized my time more?

_____

_____

What did I learn?

_____

_____

How will I improve next week?

_____

_____

Reflections:

_____

_____

I am
loved.

date: __/__/__

Sleep Tracker: _____ hours

S M T W T F S

Mood Tracker:

Today's Affirmation:

What am I looking forward to?

My top 3 to-dos:                                    Done

1.

2.

3.

What will it take to get these done?

I am grateful for:

date: ___/___/___

Rate my day: ☆ ☆ ☆ ☆ ☆

S M T W T F S

My favorite part of the day was...

_____

One thing I would change is...

_____

I am going to refill my cup by...

_____

_____

What I'll do tonight to prepare for tomorrow...

_____

_____

Tomorrow's morning routine will look like:

In bed by:_____     Alarm set for: _____

date: __/__/__

Sleep Tracker: _____ hours

S M T W T F S

Mood Tracker: 🙂 😐 🙁 😖

Today's Affirmation:

What am I looking forward to?

_____

_____

My top 3 to-dos:                                    Done

1. _____  ☐

2. _____  ☐

3. _____  ☐

What will it take to get these done?

_____

_____

I am grateful for:

_____

_____

☾

date: ___ / ___ / ___

Rate my day: ☆ ☆ ☆ ☆ ☆                    S  M  T  W  T  F  S

My favorite part of the day was...

_____

One thing I would change is...

_____

I am going to refill my cup by...

_____

_____

What I'll do tonight to prepare for tomorrow...

_____

_____

Tomorrow's morning routine will look like:

In bed by:_____    Alarm set for: _____

date: __/__/__

Sleep Tracker: _____ hours

Mood Tracker:

Today's Affirmation:

S M T W T F S

What am I looking forward to?

_____

_____

My top 3 to-dos:                                    Done

1. _____ ☐

2. _____ ☐

3. _____ ☐

What will it take to get these done?

_____

_____

I am grateful for:

_____

_____

date: ___/___/___

Rate my day: ☆ ☆ ☆ ☆ ☆          S  M  T  W  T  F  S

My favorite part of the day was...

_____

One thing I would change is...

_____

I am going to refill my cup by...

_____

_____

What I'll do tonight to prepare for tomorrow...

_____

_____

Tomorrow's morning routine will look like:

In bed by:_____    Alarm set for:_____

date: __/__/__

Sleep Tracker: _____ hours

S M T W T F S

Mood Tracker: 😊 😐 🙁 😣

Today's Affirmation:

What am I looking forward to?

_____

_____

My top 3 to-dos:                                    Done

1. _____ ☐

2. _____ ☐

3. _____ ☐

What will it take to get these done?

_____

_____

I am grateful for:

_____

_____

date: ___/___/___

Rate my day: ☆ ☆ ☆ ☆ ☆

S M T W T F S

My favorite part of the day was...

_____

One thing I would change is...

_____

I am going to refill my cup by...

_____

_____

What I'll do tonight to prepare for tomorrow...

_____

_____

Tomorrow's morning routine will look like:

In bed by:_____     Alarm set for: _____

date: __/__/__

Sleep Tracker: _____ hours

S M T W T F S

Mood Tracker: 🙂 😐 🙁 😫

Today's Affirmation:

What am I looking forward to?

_____

_____

My top 3 to-dos:                          Done

1. _____ ☐

2. _____ ☐

3. _____ ☐

What will it take to get these done?

_____

_____

I am grateful for:

_____

_____

☽

Rate my day: ☆ ☆ ☆ ☆ ☆        S M T W T F S

My favorite part of the day was...

_____

One thing I would change is...

_____

I am going to refill my cup by...

_____

_____

What I'll do tonight to prepare for tomorrow...

_____

_____

Tomorrow's morning routine will look like:

┌───────────────────────────────────────────────┐
│                                                 │
│                                                 │
│                                                 │
│                                                 │
│                                                 │
│                                                 │
└───────────────────────────────────────────────┘

In bed by:_____    Alarm set for: _____

date: __/__/__

Sleep Tracker: _____ hours

S  M  T  W  T  F  S

Mood Tracker:  ☺  😐  ☹  😠

### Today's Affirmation:

What am I looking forward to?

_____

_____

My top 3 to-dos:                          Done

1. _____  ☐

2. _____  ☐

3. _____  ☐

What will it take to get these done?

_____

_____

I am grateful for:

_____

_____

date: __/__/__

Rate my day: ☆ ☆ ☆ ☆ ☆

S M T W T F S

My favorite part of the day was...

_____

One thing I would change is...

_____

I am going to refill my cup by...

_____

_____

What I'll do tonight to prepare for tomorrow...

_____

_____

Tomorrow's morning routine will look like:

In bed by:_____     Alarm set for:_____

date: __/__/__

Sleep Tracker: _____ hours

S M T W T F S

Mood Tracker: ☺ ☹ ☹ ☹

Today's Affirmation:

What am I looking forward to?

_____

_____

My top 3 to-dos:                          Done

1. _____  ☐

2. _____  ☐

3. _____  ☐

What will it take to get these done?

_____

_____

I am grateful for:

_____

_____

date: ___/___/___

Rate my day: ☆ ☆ ☆ ☆ ☆

S M T W T F S

My favorite part of the day was...

_____

One thing I would change is...

_____

I am going to refill my cup by...

_____

_____

What I'll do tonight to prepare for tomorrow...

_____

_____

Tomorrow's morning routine will look like:

In bed by:_____     Alarm set for: _____

# Weekly Recap

date: ___/___/___

I feel...

Healthy   Accomplished   Spiritual   Creative   Satisfied

What did I do that helped me make the best use of my time?

_____

_____

How could I have maximized my time more?

_____

_____

What did I learn?

_____

_____

How will I improve next week?

_____

_____

Reflections:

_____

_____

I am
whole.

date: ___/___/___

Sleep Tracker: _____ hours

S M T W T F S

Mood Tracker: ☺ 😐 ☹ 😣

Today's Affirmation:

What am I looking forward to?

_____

_____

My top 3 to-dos:                                    Done

1. _____  ☐

2. _____  ☐

3. _____  ☐

What will it take to get these done?

_____

_____

I am grateful for:

_____

_____

☾

date: ___/___/___

Rate my day: ☆ ☆ ☆ ☆ ☆          S M T W T F S

My favorite part of the day was...

_____

One thing I would change is...

_____

I am going to refill my cup by...

_____

_____

What I'll do tonight to prepare for tomorrow...

_____

_____

Tomorrow's morning routine will look like:

In bed by:_____     Alarm set for: _____

date: __/__/__

Sleep Tracker: _____ hours

S M T W T F S

Mood Tracker: ☺ 😐 ☹ 😣

Today's Affirmation:

What am I looking forward to?

_____

_____

My top 3 to-dos:                                    Done

1. _____  ☐

2. _____  ☐

3. _____  ☐

What will it take to get these done?

_____

_____

I am grateful for:

_____

_____

Rate my day: ☆ ☆ ☆ ☆ ☆

date: ___/___/___

S M T W T F S

My favorite part of the day was...

_____

One thing I would change is...

_____

I am going to refill my cup by...

_____

_____

What I'll do tonight to prepare for tomorrow...

_____

_____

Tomorrow's morning routine will look like:

In bed by:_____    Alarm set for: _____

date: __/__/__

Sleep Tracker: _____ hours

S M T W T F S

Mood Tracker: 🙂 😐 🙁 😫

Today's Affirmation:

What am I looking forward to?

_____

_____

My top 3 to-dos:                          Done

1. _____     ☐

2. _____     ☐

3. _____     ☐

What will it take to get these done?

_____

_____

I am grateful for:

_____

_____

date: __/__/__

Rate my day: ☆ ☆ ☆ ☆ ☆

S M T W T F S

My favorite part of the day was...

_____

One thing I would change is...

_____

I am going to refill my cup by...

_____

_____

What I'll do tonight to prepare for tomorrow...

_____

_____

Tomorrow's morning routine will look like:

In bed by:_____    Alarm set for: _____

date: ___/___/___

Sleep Tracker: _____ hours

S M T W T F S

Mood Tracker: ☺ 😐 ☹ 😣

Today's Affirmation:

What am I looking forward to?

_____

_____

My top 3 to-dos:                              Done

1. _____  ☐

2. _____  ☐

3. _____  ☐

What will it take to get these done?

_____

_____

I am grateful for:

_____

_____

Rate my day: ☆ ☆ ☆ ☆ ☆          S M T W T F S

My favorite part of the day was...

_____

One thing I would change is...

_____

I am going to refill my cup by...

_____

_____

What I'll do tonight to prepare for tomorrow...

_____

_____

Tomorrow's morning routine will look like:

In bed by:_____     Alarm set for: _____

date: ___/___/___

Sleep Tracker: _____ hours

S M T W T F S

Mood Tracker: 🙂 😐 🙁 😣

### Today's Affirmation:

What am I looking forward to?

_____

_____

My top 3 to-dos:                                              Done

1. _____  ☐

2. _____  ☐

3. _____  ☐

What will it take to get these done?

_____

_____

I am grateful for:

_____

_____

Rate my day: ☆ ☆ ☆ ☆ ☆

S M T W T F S

My favorite part of the day was...

_____

One thing I would change is...

_____

I am going to refill my cup by...

_____

_____

What I'll do tonight to prepare for tomorrow...

_____

_____

Tomorrow's morning routine will look like:

In bed by:_____    Alarm set for:_____

date: ___/___/___

Sleep Tracker: _____ hours

S  M  T  W  T  F  S

Mood Tracker:  ☺  😐  🙁  😣

### Today's Affirmation:

What am I looking forward to?

_____

_____

My top 3 to-dos:                                    Done

1. _____  ☐

2. _____  ☐

3. _____  ☐

What will it take to get these done?

_____

_____

I am grateful for:

_____

_____

date: __/__/__

Rate my day: ☆ ☆ ☆ ☆ ☆

S M T W T F S

My favorite part of the day was...

_____

One thing I would change is...

_____

I am going to refill my cup by...

_____

_____

What I'll do tonight to prepare for tomorrow...

_____

_____

Tomorrow's morning routine will look like:

In bed by:_____     Alarm set for:_____

date: ___/___/___

Sleep Tracker: _____ hours

S M T W T F S

Mood Tracker: ☺ 😐 ☹ 😣

## Today's Affirmation:

What am I looking forward to?

_____

_____

My top 3 to-dos:                                    Done

1. _____  ☐

2. _____  ☐

3. _____  ☐

What will it take to get these done?

_____

_____

I am grateful for:

_____

_____

date: ___/___/___

Rate my day: ☆ ☆ ☆ ☆ ☆

S M T W T F S

My favorite part of the day was...

_____

One thing I would change is...

_____

I am going to refill my cup by...

_____

_____

What I'll do tonight to prepare for tomorrow...

_____

_____

Tomorrow's morning routine will look like:

In bed by:_____ Alarm set for:_____

# Weekly Recap

date: ___/___/___

I feel...

Healthy   Accomplished   Spiritual   Creative   Satisfied

What did I do that helped me make the best use of my time?

_____

_____

How could I have maximized my time more?

_____

_____

What did I learn?

_____

_____

How will I improve next week?

_____

_____

Reflections:

_____

_____

I am
disciplined.

date: ___/___/___

Sleep Tracker: _____ hours

S M T W T F S

Mood Tracker: ☺ 😐 ☹ 😣

Today's Affirmation:

What am I looking forward to?

_____

_____

My top 3 to-dos:                                    Done

1. _____  ☐

2. _____  ☐

3. _____  ☐

What will it take to get these done?

_____

_____

I am grateful for:

_____

_____

Rate my day: ☆ ☆ ☆ ☆ ☆

My favorite part of the day was...

_____

One thing I would change is...

_____

I am going to refill my cup by...

_____

_____

What I'll do tonight to prepare for tomorrow...

_____

_____

Tomorrow's morning routine will look like:

[ ]

In bed by:_____    Alarm set for: _____

date: ___/___/___

Sleep Tracker: _____ hours

S  M  T  W  T  F  S

Mood Tracker:  ☺  😐  🙁  😫

## Today's Affirmation:

What am I looking forward to?

_____

_____

My top 3 to-dos:                                    Done

1. _____  ☐

2. _____  ☐

3. _____  ☐

What will it take to get these done?

_____

_____

I am grateful for:

_____

_____

Rate my day: ☆ ☆ ☆ ☆ ☆

My favorite part of the day was...

_____

One thing I would change is...

_____

I am going to refill my cup by...

_____

_____

What I'll do tonight to prepare for tomorrow...

_____

_____

Tomorrow's morning routine will look like:

In bed by:_____    Alarm set for: _____

date: __/__/__

Sleep Tracker: _____ hours

S M T W T F S

Mood Tracker: ☺ 😐 ☹ 😣

## Today's Affirmation:

What am I looking forward to?

_____

_____

My top 3 to-dos: Done

1. _____ ☐

2. _____ ☐

3. _____ ☐

What will it take to get these done?

_____

_____

I am grateful for:

_____

_____

☾

Rate my day: ☆ ☆ ☆ ☆ ☆

S M T W T F S

My favorite part of the day was...

_____

One thing I would change is...

_____

I am going to refill my cup by...

_____

_____

What I'll do tonight to prepare for tomorrow...

_____

_____

Tomorrow's morning routine will look like:

In bed by:_____   Alarm set for: _____

date: ___/___/___

Sleep Tracker: _____ hours

S  M  T  W  T  F  S

Mood Tracker: ☺ 😐 🙁 😖

## Today's Affirmation:

What am I looking forward to?

_____

_____

My top 3 to-dos:                                     Done

1. _____  ☐

2. _____  ☐

3. _____  ☐

What will it take to get these done?

_____

_____

I am grateful for:

_____

_____

date: __/__/__

Rate my day: ☆ ☆ ☆ ☆ ☆

S M T W T F S

My favorite part of the day was...

_____

One thing I would change is...

_____

I am going to refill my cup by...

_____

_____

What I'll do tonight to prepare for tomorrow...

_____

_____

Tomorrow's morning routine will look like:

In bed by:_____     Alarm set for:_____

date: __/__/__

Sleep Tracker: _____ hours

S M T W T F S

Mood Tracker:

Today's Affirmation:

What am I looking forward to?

My top 3 to-dos:                                    Done

1.

2.

3.

What will it take to get these done?

I am grateful for:

date: __/__/__

Rate my day: ☆ ☆ ☆ ☆ ☆

S M T W T F S

My favorite part of the day was...

_____

One thing I would change is...

_____

I am going to refill my cup by...

_____

_____

What I'll do tonight to prepare for tomorrow...

_____

_____

Tomorrow's morning routine will look like:

In bed by:_____    Alarm set for: _____

date: ___/___/___

Sleep Tracker: _____ hours

S M T W T F S

Mood Tracker: 🙂 😐 🙁 😣

Today's Affirmation:

What am I looking forward to?

_____

_____

My top 3 to-dos:                                        Done

1. _____  ☐

2. _____  ☐

3. _____  ☐

What will it take to get these done?

_____

_____

I am grateful for:

_____

_____

☾

Rate my day: ☆ ☆ ☆ ☆ ☆

S M T W T F S

My favorite part of the day was...

_____

One thing I would change is...

_____

I am going to refill my cup by...

_____

_____

What I'll do tonight to prepare for tomorrow...

_____

_____

Tomorrow's morning routine will look like:

In bed by:_____    Alarm set for: _____

date: __/__/__

Sleep Tracker: _____ hours

S M T W T F S

Mood Tracker: 🙂 😐 🙁 😫

Today's Affirmation:

What am I looking forward to?

_____

_____

My top 3 to-dos:                    Done

1. _____ ☐

2. _____ ☐

3. _____ ☐

What will it take to get these done?

_____

_____

I am grateful for:

_____

_____

☾

Rate my day: ☆ ☆ ☆ ☆ ☆

S M T W T F S

My favorite part of the day was...

_____

One thing I would change is...

_____

I am going to refill my cup by...

_____

_____

What I'll do tonight to prepare for tomorrow...

_____

_____

Tomorrow's morning routine will look like:

In bed by:_____    Alarm set for: _____

# Weekly Recap

date: ___/___/___

I feel...

Healthy  Accomplished  Spiritual  Creative  Satisfied

What did I do that helped me make the best use of my time?

_____

_____

How could I have maximized my time more?

_____

_____

What did I learn?

_____

_____

How will I improve next week?

_____

_____

Reflections:

_____

_____

I am
prepared.

date: __/__/__

Sleep Tracker: _____ hours

S M T W T F S

Mood Tracker: ☺ 😐 🙁 😣

Today's Affirmation:

What am I looking forward to?

My top 3 to-dos:                                    Done

1. _____  ☐

2. _____  ☐

3. _____  ☐

What will it take to get these done?

I am grateful for:

date: __/__/__

Rate my day: ☆☆☆☆☆

S M T W T F S

My favorite part of the day was...

_____

One thing I would change is...

_____

I am going to refill my cup by...

_____

_____

What I'll do tonight to prepare for tomorrow...

_____

_____

Tomorrow's morning routine will look like:

In bed by:____    Alarm set for: ____

date: ___/___/___

Sleep Tracker: _____ hours

S M T W T F S

Mood Tracker:

Today's Affirmation:

What am I looking forward to?

_____

_____

My top 3 to-dos:                    Done

1. _____ ☐

2. _____ ☐

3. _____ ☐

What will it take to get these done?

_____

_____

I am grateful for:

_____

_____

date: __/__/__

Rate my day: ☆ ☆ ☆ ☆ ☆

S M T W T F S

My favorite part of the day was...

_____

One thing I would change is...

_____

I am going to refill my cup by...

_____

_____

What I'll do tonight to prepare for tomorrow...

_____

_____

Tomorrow's morning routine will look like:

In bed by:_____    Alarm set for: _____

date: __/__/__

Sleep Tracker: _____ hours

S M T W T F S

Mood Tracker: 😊 😐 🙁 😣

Today's Affirmation:

What am I looking forward to?

My top 3 to-dos:                                              Done

1.                                                            ☐

2.                                                            ☐

3.                                                            ☐

What will it take to get these done?

I am grateful for:

☽

Rate my day: ☆ ☆ ☆ ☆ ☆          S M T W T F S

My favorite part of the day was...

_____

One thing I would change is...

_____

I am going to refill my cup by...

_____

_____

What I'll do tonight to prepare for tomorrow...

_____

_____

Tomorrow's morning routine will look like:

In bed by:_____    Alarm set for:_____

date: __/__/__

Sleep Tracker: _____ hours

S M T W T F S

Mood Tracker: 😊 😐 🙁 😠

Today's Affirmation:

What am I looking forward to?

_____

_____

My top 3 to-dos:                    Done

1. _____  ☐

2. _____  ☐

3. _____  ☐

What will it take to get these done?

_____

_____

I am grateful for:

_____

_____

date: __/__/__

Rate my day: ☆ ☆ ☆ ☆ ☆

S M T W T F S

My favorite part of the day was...

_____

One thing I would change is...

_____

I am going to refill my cup by...

_____

_____

What I'll do tonight to prepare for tomorrow...

_____

_____

Tomorrow's morning routine will look like:

In bed by:_____ Alarm set for: _____

date: __ / __ / __

Sleep Tracker: _____ hours

S  M  T  W  T  F  S

Mood Tracker: 😊 😐 🙁 😠

### Today's Affirmation:

What am I looking forward to?

My top 3 to-dos:                    Done

1. _____  ☐

2. _____  ☐

3. _____  ☐

What will it take to get these done?

I am grateful for:

date: ___/___/___

Rate my day: ☆ ☆ ☆ ☆ ☆

S M T W T F S

My favorite part of the day was...

_____

One thing I would change is...

_____

I am going to refill my cup by...

_____

_____

What I'll do tonight to prepare for tomorrow...

_____

_____

Tomorrow's morning routine will look like:

In bed by:_____     Alarm set for: _____

date: __/__/__

Sleep Tracker: _____ hours

S M T W T F S

Mood Tracker: ☺ 😐 ☹ 😠

### Today's Affirmation:

What am I looking forward to?

_____

_____

My top 3 to-dos:                                    Done

1. _____  ☐

2. _____  ☐

3. _____  ☐

What will it take to get these done?

_____

_____

I am grateful for:

_____

_____

☾

Rate my day: ☆ ☆ ☆ ☆ ☆

S M T W T F S

My favorite part of the day was...

_____

One thing I would change is...

_____

I am going to refill my cup by...

_____

_____

What I'll do tonight to prepare for tomorrow...

_____

_____

Tomorrow's morning routine will look like:

In bed by:_____    Alarm set for: _____

date: __/__/__

Sleep Tracker: _____ hours

S M T W T F S

Mood Tracker: ☺ 😐 ☹ 😠

Today's Affirmation:

What am I looking forward to?

_____

_____

My top 3 to-dos:                                    Done

1. _____  ☐

2. _____  ☐

3. _____  ☐

What will it take to get these done?

_____

_____

I am grateful for:

_____

_____

Rate my day: ☆ ☆ ☆ ☆ ☆

S M T W T F S

My favorite part of the day was...

_____

One thing I would change is...

_____

I am going to refill my cup by...

_____

_____

What I'll do tonight to prepare for tomorrow...

_____

_____

Tomorrow's morning routine will look like:

In bed by:_____    Alarm set for: _____

# Weekly Recap

date: ___/___/___

I feel...

Healthy   Accomplished   Spiritual   Creative   Satisfied

What did I do that helped me make the best use of
my time?

_____

_____

How could I have maximized my time more?

_____

_____

What did I learn?

_____

_____

How will I improve next week?

_____

_____

Reflections:

_____

_____

I am
purposeful.

date: ___/___/___

Sleep Tracker: _____ hours

S M T W T F S

Mood Tracker: ☺ 😐 ☹ 😠

### Today's Affirmation:

What am I looking forward to?

_____

_____

My top 3 to-dos:                                    Done

1. _____ ☐

2. _____ ☐

3. _____ ☐

What will it take to get these done?

_____

_____

I am grateful for:

_____

_____

date: ___/___/___

Rate my day: ☆ ☆ ☆ ☆ ☆

S M T W T F S

My favorite part of the day was...

_____

One thing I would change is...

_____

I am going to refill my cup by...

_____

_____

What I'll do tonight to prepare for tomorrow...

_____

_____

Tomorrow's morning routine will look like:

In bed by:_____     Alarm set for: _____

date: ___/___/___

Sleep Tracker: _____ hours

S  M  T  W  T  F  S

Mood Tracker:  🙂  😐  🙁  😠

### Today's Affirmation:

What am I looking forward to?

_____

_____

My top 3 to-dos:                                    Done

1. _____  ☐

2. _____  ☐

3. _____  ☐

What will it take to get these done?

_____

_____

I am grateful for:

_____

_____

date: __/__/__

Rate my day: ☆ ☆ ☆ ☆ ☆

S M T W T F S

My favorite part of the day was...

_____

One thing I would change is...

_____

I am going to refill my cup by...

_____

_____

What I'll do tonight to prepare for tomorrow...

_____

_____

Tomorrow's morning routine will look like:

In bed by:_____    Alarm set for: _____

date: ___/___/___

Sleep Tracker: _____ hours

S M T W T F S

Mood Tracker: 🙂 😐 🙁 😫

Today's Affirmation:

What am I looking forward to?

_____

_____

My top 3 to-dos:                                    Done

1. _____            ☐

2. _____            ☐

3. _____            ☐

What will it take to get these done?

_____

_____

I am grateful for:

_____

_____

date: __/__/__

Rate my day: ☆☆☆☆☆

S M T W T F S

My favorite part of the day was...

_____

One thing I would change is...

_____

I am going to refill my cup by...

_____

_____

What I'll do tonight to prepare for tomorrow...

_____

_____

Tomorrow's morning routine will look like:

In bed by:_____    Alarm set for: _____

date: __/__/__

Sleep Tracker: _____ hours

S M T W T F S

Mood Tracker:

Today's Affirmation:

What am I looking forward to?

My top 3 to-dos:                                    Done

1.

2.

3.

What will it take to get these done?

I am grateful for:

date: __/__/__

Rate my day: ☆☆☆☆☆

S M T W T F S

My favorite part of the day was...

_____

One thing I would change is...

_____

I am going to refill my cup by...

_____

_____

What I'll do tonight to prepare for tomorrow...

_____

_____

Tomorrow's morning routine will look like:

In bed by:_____    Alarm set for: _____

date: ___/___/___

Sleep Tracker: _____ hours

S  M  T  W  T  F  S

Mood Tracker: 🙂 😐 🙁 😣

### Today's Affirmation:

What am I looking forward to?

_____

_____

My top 3 to-dos:                                      Done

1. _____  ☐

2. _____  ☐

3. _____  ☐

What will it take to get these done?

_____

_____

I am grateful for:

_____

_____

date: __/__/__

Rate my day: ☆ ☆ ☆ ☆ ☆

S M T W T F S

My favorite part of the day was...

_____

One thing I would change is...

_____

I am going to refill my cup by...

_____

_____

What I'll do tonight to prepare for tomorrow...

_____

_____

Tomorrow's morning routine will look like:

In bed by:_____    Alarm set for: _____

date: ___/___/___

Sleep Tracker: _____ hours

S M T W T F S

Mood Tracker: ☺ 😐 ☹ 😠

Today's Affirmation:

What am I looking forward to?

_____

_____

My top 3 to-dos:                                      Done

1. _____ ☐

2. _____ ☐

3. _____ ☐

What will it take to get these done?

_____

_____

I am grateful for:

_____

_____

Rate my day: ☆ ☆ ☆ ☆ ☆

My favorite part of the day was...

_____

One thing I would change is...

_____

I am going to refill my cup by...

_____

_____

What I'll do tonight to prepare for tomorrow...

_____

_____

Tomorrow's morning routine will look like:

In bed by:_____    Alarm set for: _____

date: ___/___/___

Sleep Tracker: _____ hours

S  M  T  W  T  F  S

Mood Tracker:

Today's Affirmation:

What am I looking forward to?

My top 3 to-dos:                                             Done

1. _____  ☐

2. _____  ☐

3. _____  ☐

What will it take to get these done?

I am grateful for:

date: ___/___/___

Rate my day: ☆ ☆ ☆ ☆ ☆

S M T W T F S

My favorite part of the day was...

_____

One thing I would change is...

_____

I am going to refill my cup by...

_____

_____

What I'll do tonight to prepare for tomorrow...

_____

_____

Tomorrow's morning routine will look like:

In bed by:_____    Alarm set for: _____

# Weekly Recap

date: ___/___/___

I feel...

Healthy   Accomplished   Spiritual   Creative   Satisfied

What did I do that helped me make the best use of my time?

_____

_____

How could I have maximized my time more?

_____

_____

What did I learn?

_____

_____

How will I improve next week?

_____

_____

Reflections:

_____

_____

I am
inspired.

date: __/__/__

Sleep Tracker: _____ hours

S M T W T F S

Mood Tracker: 😊 😐 🙁 😣

### Today's Affirmation:

|  |
|--|
|  |

## What am I looking forward to?

_____

_____

## My top 3 to-dos:                                      Done

1. _____  ☐

2. _____  ☐

3. _____  ☐

## What will it take to get these done?

_____

_____

## I am grateful for:

_____

_____

☾

Rate my day: ☆ ☆ ☆ ☆ ☆          S M T W T F S

My favorite part of the day was...

_____

One thing I would change is...

_____

I am going to refill my cup by...

_____

_____

What I'll do tonight to prepare for tomorrow...

_____

_____

Tomorrow's morning routine will look like:

In bed by:_____     Alarm set for: _____

date: __/__/__

Sleep Tracker: _____ hours

S M T W T F S

Mood Tracker:  ☺ 😐 ☹ 😠

### Today's Affirmation:

What am I looking forward to?

_____

_____

My top 3 to-dos:                              Done

1. _____  ☐

2. _____  ☐

3. _____  ☐

What will it take to get these done?

_____

_____

I am grateful for:

_____

_____

date: __/__/__

Rate my day: ☆☆☆☆☆

S M T W T F S

My favorite part of the day was...

_____

One thing I would change is...

_____

I am going to refill my cup by...

_____

_____

What I'll do tonight to prepare for tomorrow...

_____

_____

Tomorrow's morning routine will look like:

In bed by:_____     Alarm set for: _____

date: __/__/__

Sleep Tracker: _____ hours

S M T W T F S

Mood Tracker: ☺ 😐 ☹ 😖

### Today's Affirmation:

What am I looking forward to?

My top 3 to-dos:                                          Done

1. _____  ☐

2. _____  ☐

3. _____  ☐

What will it take to get these done?

I am grateful for:

date: ___/___/___

Rate my day: ☆☆☆☆☆

S M T W T F S

My favorite part of the day was...

_____

One thing I would change is...

_____

I am going to refill my cup by...

_____

_____

What I'll do tonight to prepare for tomorrow...

_____

_____

Tomorrow's morning routine will look like:

In bed by:_____     Alarm set for: _____

date: __/__/__

Sleep Tracker: _____ hours

S M T W T F S

Mood Tracker: ☺ 😐 ☹ 😠

## Today's Affirmation:

What am I looking forward to?

_____

_____

My top 3 to-dos:                    Done

1. _____  ☐

2. _____  ☐

3. _____  ☐

What will it take to get these done?

_____

_____

I am grateful for:

_____

_____

date: ___/___/___

Rate my day: ☆☆☆☆☆

S M T W T F S

My favorite part of the day was...

_____

One thing I would change is...

_____

I am going to refill my cup by...

_____

_____

What I'll do tonight to prepare for tomorrow...

_____

_____

Tomorrow's morning routine will look like:

In bed by:_____    Alarm set for: _____

date: __/__/__

Sleep Tracker: _____ hours

S M T W T F S

Mood Tracker: ☺ 😐 🙁 😣

Today's Affirmation:

What am I looking forward to?

_____

_____

My top 3 to-dos:                                    Done

1. _____  ☐

2. _____  ☐

3. _____  ☐

What will it take to get these done?

_____

_____

I am grateful for:

_____

_____

☾

date: __/__/__

Rate my day: ☆☆☆☆☆

S M T W T F S

My favorite part of the day was...

_____

One thing I would change is...

_____

I am going to refill my cup by...

_____

_____

What I'll do tonight to prepare for tomorrow...

_____

_____

Tomorrow's morning routine will look like:

In bed by:_____    Alarm set for: _____

date: ___/___/___

Sleep Tracker: _____ hours

S  M  T  W  T  F  S

Mood Tracker: ☺ 😐 ☹ 😠

## Today's Affirmation:

What am I looking forward to?

_____

_____

My top 3 to-dos:                    Done

1. _____ ☐

2. _____ ☐

3. _____ ☐

What will it take to get these done?

_____

_____

I am grateful for:

_____

_____

date: ___/___/___

Rate my day: ☆ ☆ ☆ ☆ ☆

S M T W T F S

My favorite part of the day was...

_____

One thing I would change is...

_____

I am going to refill my cup by...

_____

_____

What I'll do tonight to prepare for tomorrow...

_____

_____

Tomorrow's morning routine will look like:

In bed by:_____     Alarm set for: _____

date: ___/___/___

Sleep Tracker: _____ hours

S  M  T  W  T  F  S

Mood Tracker: ☺ 😐 🙁 😣

### Today's Affirmation:

What am I looking forward to?

_____

_____

My top 3 to-dos:                                    Done

1. _____  ☐

2. _____  ☐

3. _____  ☐

What will it take to get these done?

_____

_____

I am grateful for:

_____

_____

Rate my day: ☆ ☆ ☆ ☆ ☆

date: ___/___/___

S M T W T F S

My favorite part of the day was...

_____

One thing I would change is...

_____

I am going to refill my cup by...

_____

_____

What I'll do tonight to prepare for tomorrow...

_____

_____

Tomorrow's morning routine will look like:

In bed by:_____     Alarm set for: _____

*Weekly Recap*                          date: ___/___/___

I feel...

Healthy   Accomplished   Spiritual   Creative   Satisfied

What did I do that helped me make the best use of
my time?

_____

_____

How could I have maximized my time more?

_____

_____

What did I learn?

_____

_____

How will I improve next week?

_____

_____

Reflections:

_____

_____

I am
empowered.

date: __/__/__

Sleep Tracker: _____ hours

S M T W T F S

Mood Tracker: 😊 😐 🙁 😣

### Today's Affirmation:

What am I looking forward to?

My top 3 to-dos:                                      Done

1. _____  ☐

2. _____  ☐

3. _____  ☐

What will it take to get these done?

I am grateful for:

Rate my day: ☆ ☆ ☆ ☆ ☆          S M T W T F S

My favorite part of the day was...

_____

One thing I would change is...

_____

I am going to refill my cup by...

_____

_____

What I'll do tonight to prepare for tomorrow...

_____

_____

Tomorrow's morning routine will look like:

In bed by:_____     Alarm set for: _____

date: __/__/__

Sleep Tracker: _____ hours

S M T W T F S

Mood Tracker: 😊 😐 ☹️ 😖

## Today's Affirmation:

What am I looking forward to?

_____

_____

My top 3 to-dos:                    Done

1. _____  ☐

2. _____  ☐

3. _____  ☐

What will it take to get these done?

_____

_____

I am grateful for:

_____

_____

☾

date: __/__/__

Rate my day: ☆ ☆ ☆ ☆ ☆

S M T W T F S

My favorite part of the day was...

_____

One thing I would change is...

_____

I am going to refill my cup by...

_____

_____

What I'll do tonight to prepare for tomorrow...

_____

_____

Tomorrow's morning routine will look like:

In bed by:_____     Alarm set for: _____

date: ___/___/___

Sleep Tracker: _____ hours

S M T W T F S

Mood Tracker: ☺ ☺ ☹ ☹

### Today's Affirmation:

What am I looking forward to?

_____

_____

My top 3 to-dos:                    Done

1. _____  ☐

2. _____  ☐

3. _____  ☐

What will it take to get these done?

_____

_____

I am grateful for:

_____

_____

date: ___/___/___

Rate my day: ☆ ☆ ☆ ☆ ☆

S M T W T F S

My favorite part of the day was...

_____

One thing I would change is...

_____

I am going to refill my cup by...

_____

_____

What I'll do tonight to prepare for tomorrow...

_____

_____

Tomorrow's morning routine will look like:

In bed by:_____     Alarm set for: _____

date: __/__/__

Sleep Tracker: _____ hours

S  M  T  W  T  F  S

Mood Tracker:

Today's Affirmation:

What am I looking forward to?

My top 3 to-dos:                                    Done

1. _____    ☐

2. _____    ☐

3. _____    ☐

What will it take to get these done?

I am grateful for:

Rate my day: ☆ ☆ ☆ ☆ ☆

date: __/__/__

S M T W T F S

My favorite part of the day was...

_____

One thing I would change is...

_____

I am going to refill my cup by...

_____

_____

What I'll do tonight to prepare for tomorrow...

_____

_____

Tomorrow's morning routine will look like:

In bed by:_____    Alarm set for: _____

date: ___/___/___

Sleep Tracker: _____ hours

S M T W T F S

Mood Tracker: 🙂 😐 ☹️ 😣

Today's Affirmation:

What am I looking forward to?

_____

_____

My top 3 to-dos:                          Done

1.
_____          ☐

2.
_____          ☐

3.
_____          ☐

What will it take to get these done?

_____

_____

I am grateful for:

_____

_____

☾

Rate my day: ☆ ☆ ☆ ☆ ☆          S  M  T  W  T  F  S

My favorite part of the day was...

_____

One thing I would change is...

_____

I am going to refill my cup by...

_____

_____

What I'll do tonight to prepare for tomorrow...

_____

_____

Tomorrow's morning routine will look like:

In bed by:_____     Alarm set for: _____

date: \_\_/\_\_/\_\_

Sleep Tracker: \_\_\_\_\_ hours

S M T W T F S

Mood Tracker: 🙂 😐 🙁 😣

### Today's Affirmation:

What am I looking forward to?

_____

_____

My top 3 to-dos:                                    Done

1. _____    ☐

2. _____    ☐

3. _____    ☐

What will it take to get these done?

_____

_____

I am grateful for:

_____

_____

☾

date: __/__/__

Rate my day: ☆ ☆ ☆ ☆ ☆

S M T W T F S

My favorite part of the day was...

_____

One thing I would change is...

_____

I am going to refill my cup by...

_____

_____

What I'll do tonight to prepare for tomorrow...

_____

_____

Tomorrow's morning routine will look like:

In bed by:_____     Alarm set for: _____

date: __/__/__

Sleep Tracker: _____ hours

S M T W T F S

Mood Tracker: 🙂 😐 🙁 😠

## Today's Affirmation:

What am I looking forward to?

_____

_____

My top 3 to-dos:                    Done

1. _____  ☐

2. _____  ☐

3. _____  ☐

What will it take to get these done?

_____

_____

I am grateful for:

_____

_____

☾

date: ___/___/___

Rate my day: ☆ ☆ ☆ ☆ ☆

S M T W T F S

My favorite part of the day was...

_____

One thing I would change is...

_____

I am going to refill my cup by...

_____

_____

What I'll do tonight to prepare for tomorrow...

_____

_____

Tomorrow's morning routine will look like:

In bed by:_____ Alarm set for: _____

# Weekly Recap

I feel...

Healthy   Accomplished   Spiritual   Creative   Satisfied

What did I do that helped me make the best use of my time?

_____

_____

How could I have maximized my time more?

_____

_____

What did I learn?

_____

_____

How will I improve next week?

_____

_____

Reflections:

_____

_____

I am
free.

date: __/__/__

Sleep Tracker: _____ hours

S  M  T  W  T  F  S

Mood Tracker:  ☺  😐  ☹  😣

### Today's Affirmation:



What am I looking forward to?

_____

_____

My top 3 to-dos:                                    Done

1. _____  ☐

2. _____  ☐

3. _____  ☐

What will it take to get these done?

_____

_____

I am grateful for:

_____

_____

date: ___/___/___

Rate my day: ☆ ☆ ☆ ☆ ☆

S M T W T F S

My favorite part of the day was...

_____

One thing I would change is...

_____

I am going to refill my cup by...

_____

_____

What I'll do tonight to prepare for tomorrow...

_____

_____

Tomorrow's morning routine will look like:

In bed by:_____    Alarm set for: _____

date: ___/___/___

Sleep Tracker: _____ hours

S M T W T F S

Mood Tracker: 🙂 😐 🙁 😣

### Today's Affirmation:

What am I looking forward to?

_____

_____

My top 3 to-dos:                                Done

1. _____  ☐

2. _____  ☐

3. _____  ☐

What will it take to get these done?

_____

_____

I am grateful for:

_____

_____

date: __/__/__

Rate my day: ☆ ☆ ☆ ☆ ☆

S M T W T F S

My favorite part of the day was...

_____

One thing I would change is...

_____

I am going to refill my cup by...

_____

_____

What I'll do tonight to prepare for tomorrow...

_____

_____

Tomorrow's morning routine will look like:

In bed by:_____    Alarm set for: _____

date: __/__/__

Sleep Tracker: _____ hours

S M T W T F S

Mood Tracker: ☺ 😐 ☹ 😣

Today's Affirmation:

What am I looking forward to?

_____

_____

My top 3 to-dos:                                    Done

1. _____ ☐

2. _____ ☐

3. _____ ☐

What will it take to get these done?

_____

_____

I am grateful for:

_____

_____

date: ___/___/___

Rate my day: ☆ ☆ ☆ ☆ ☆

S M T W T F S

My favorite part of the day was...

_____

One thing I would change is...

_____

I am going to refill my cup by...

_____

_____

What I'll do tonight to prepare for tomorrow...

_____

_____

Tomorrow's morning routine will look like:

In bed by:_____    Alarm set for: _____

date: ___ / ___ / ___

Sleep Tracker: _____ hours

S M T W T F S

Mood Tracker: ☺ 😐 🙁 😠

Today's Affirmation:

What am I looking forward to?

_____

_____

My top 3 to-dos:                                      Done

1. _____  ☐

2. _____  ☐

3. _____  ☐

What will it take to get these done?

_____

_____

I am grateful for:

_____

_____

date: __ / __ / __

Rate my day: ☆ ☆ ☆ ☆ ☆

S M T W T F S

My favorite part of the day was...

_____

One thing I would change is...

_____

I am going to refill my cup by...

_____

_____

What I'll do tonight to prepare for tomorrow...

_____

_____

Tomorrow's morning routine will look like:

In bed by:____    Alarm set for: _____

date: __/__/__

Sleep Tracker: _____ hours

S M T W T F S

Mood Tracker: 🙂 😐 🙁 😣

### Today's Affirmation:

What am I looking forward to?

_____

_____

My top 3 to-dos:                          Done

1. _____   ☐

2. _____   ☐

3. _____   ☐

What will it take to get these done?

_____

_____

I am grateful for:

_____

_____

date: __/__/__

Rate my day: ☆ ☆ ☆ ☆ ☆

S M T W T F S

My favorite part of the day was...

_____

One thing I would change is...

_____

I am going to refill my cup by...

_____

_____

What I'll do tonight to prepare for tomorrow...

_____

_____

Tomorrow's morning routine will look like:

In bed by:_____     Alarm set for: _____

date: ___/___/___

Sleep Tracker: _____ hours

S M T W T F S

Mood Tracker: 🙂 😐 🙁 😣

Today's Affirmation:

What am I looking forward to?

_____

_____

My top 3 to-dos:                              Done

1. _____  ☐

2. _____  ☐

3. _____  ☐

What will it take to get these done?

_____

_____

I am grateful for:

_____

_____

date: __/__/__

Rate my day: ☆ ☆ ☆ ☆ ☆

S M T W T F S

My favorite part of the day was...

_____

One thing I would change is...

_____

I am going to refill my cup by...

_____

_____

What I'll do tonight to prepare for tomorrow...

_____

_____

Tomorrow's morning routine will look like:

In bed by:_____    Alarm set for:_____

date: ___/___/___

Sleep Tracker: _____ hours

S M T W T F S

Mood Tracker: 🙂 😐 🙁 😣

## Today's Affirmation:

What am I looking forward to?

_____

_____

My top 3 to-dos:                                        Done

1. _____  ☐

2. _____  ☐

3. _____  ☐

What will it take to get these done?

_____

_____

I am grateful for:

_____

_____

date: __/__/__

Rate my day: ☆ ☆ ☆ ☆ ☆

S M T W T F S

My favorite part of the day was...

_____

One thing I would change is...

_____

I am going to refill my cup by...

_____

_____

What I'll do tonight to prepare for tomorrow...

_____

_____

Tomorrow's morning routine will look like:

In bed by:_____     Alarm set for: _____

# Weekly Recap

date: __/__/__

I feel...

Healthy   Accomplished   Spiritual   Creative   Satisfied

What did I do that helped me make the best use of my time?

_____

_____

How could I have maximized my time more?

_____

_____

What did I learn?

_____

_____

How will I improve next week?

_____

_____

Reflections:

_____

_____

# Reflections

date: ___/___/___

_____

_____

_____

_____

_____

_____

_____

_____

_____

_____

_____

_____

_____

_____

# Reflections

date: ___/___/___

# Reflections

date: ___/___/___

# Reflections

date: ___/___/___

Made in the USA
Columbia, SC
07 April 2024